RED PANDAS

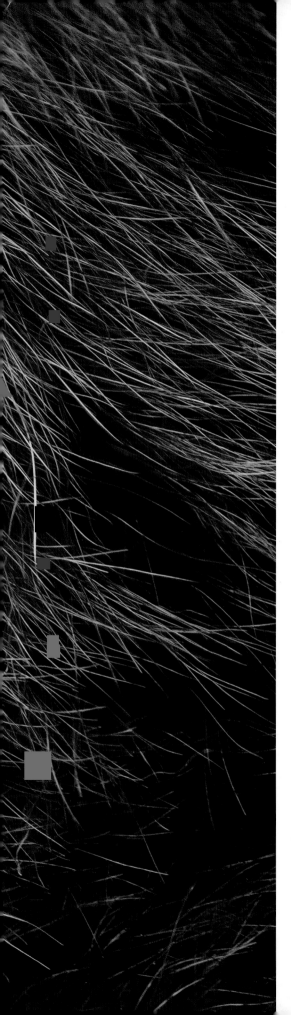

LIVING WILD

Published by Creative Education and Creative Paperbacks
P.O. Box 227, Mankato, Minnesota 56002
Creative Education and Creative Paperbacks are imprints of The Creative Company
www.thecreativecompany.us

Design and production by Mary Herrmann
Art direction by Rita Marshall
Printed in China

Photographs by Alamy (AF archive, Natural Visions), Creative Commons Wikimedia (ArindamRoy1993; Daiju Azuma/OpenCage; Peigné, S., Salesa, M.J., Antón, M., and Morales, J.), iStockphoto (kata716, raciro, ~UserGI15791109), Shutterstock (Al-Tair, Nick Biemans, Nublee bin Shamsu Bahar, Olga Bogatyrenko, Canon Boy, Hung Chung Chih, Dan Williams Photography, dangdumrong, digitalpark, esdeem, Satoru Hatakeyama, Jelena Janjetovic, Saran Jantraurai, Tao Jiang, Gail Johnson, Juhku, Thanthima Lim, mary416, Shivang Mehta, Mivr, c. mokri – austria, MyImages – Micha, Natthorn, nelik, Jay Ondreicka, praiadotofo, sebartz, Skreidzeleu, RAJU SONI, Vasin Srethaphakdi, yuribon), Smithsonian's National Zoo & Conservation Biology Institute

Library of Congress Cataloging-in-Publication Data
Names: Gish, Melissa, author.
Title: Red pandas / Melissa Gish.
Series: Living wild.
Summary: A look at red pandas, including their habitats, physical characteristics such as their long, thick fur, behaviors, relationships with humans, and the numerous threats these elusive endangered bears face today.
Identifiers: LCCN 2017038414 / ISBN 978-1-60818-960-1 (hardcover) / ISBN 978-1-62832-565-2 (pbk) / ISBN 978-1-64000-039-1 (eBook)

Subjects: LCSH: Red Panda—Juvenile literature.
Classification: LCC QL737.C214 G57 2018 / DDC 599.76/3—dc23

CCSS: RI.5.1, 2, 3, 8; RST.6-8.1, 2, 5, 6, 8; RH.6-8.3, 4, 5, 6, 7, 8

First Edition HC 9 8 7 6 5 4 3 2 1
First Edition PBK 9 8 7 6 5 4 3 2 1

CREATIVE EDUCATION • CREATIVE PAPERBACKS

RED PANDAS

Melissa Gish

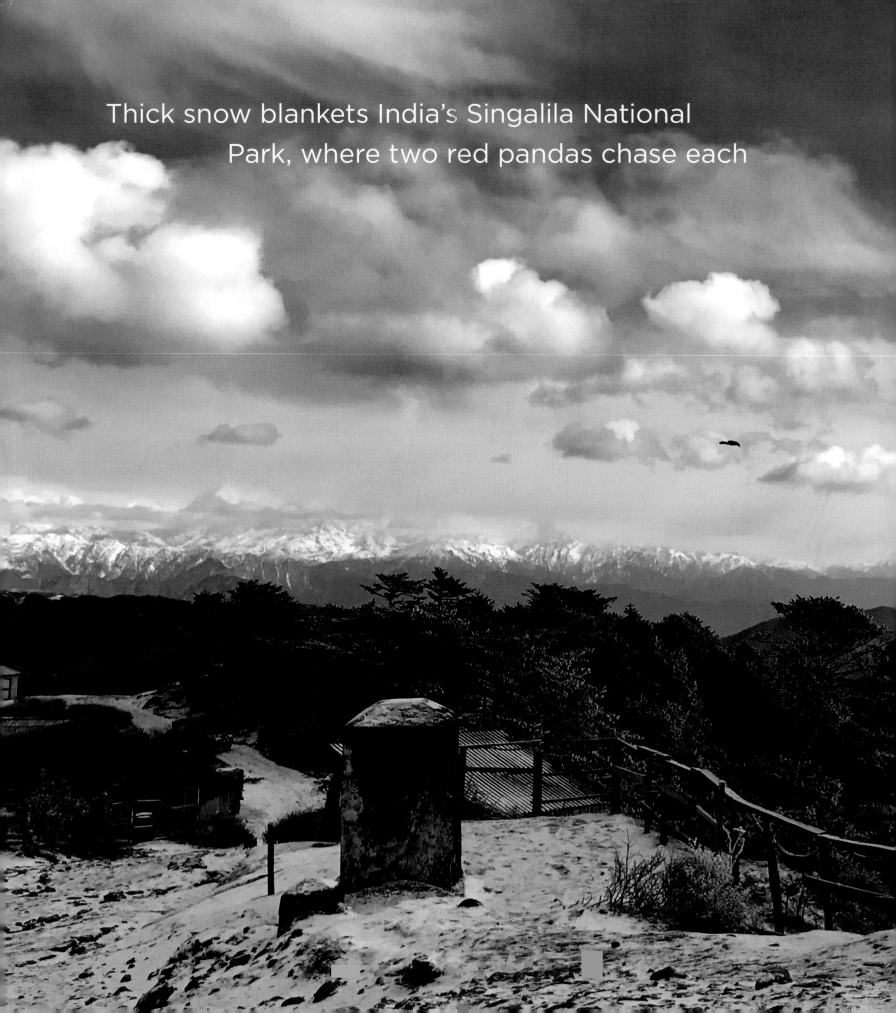

Thick snow blankets India's Singalila National Park, where two red pandas chase each

other along a high tree branch. Their bushy tails toss snow to the ground far below.

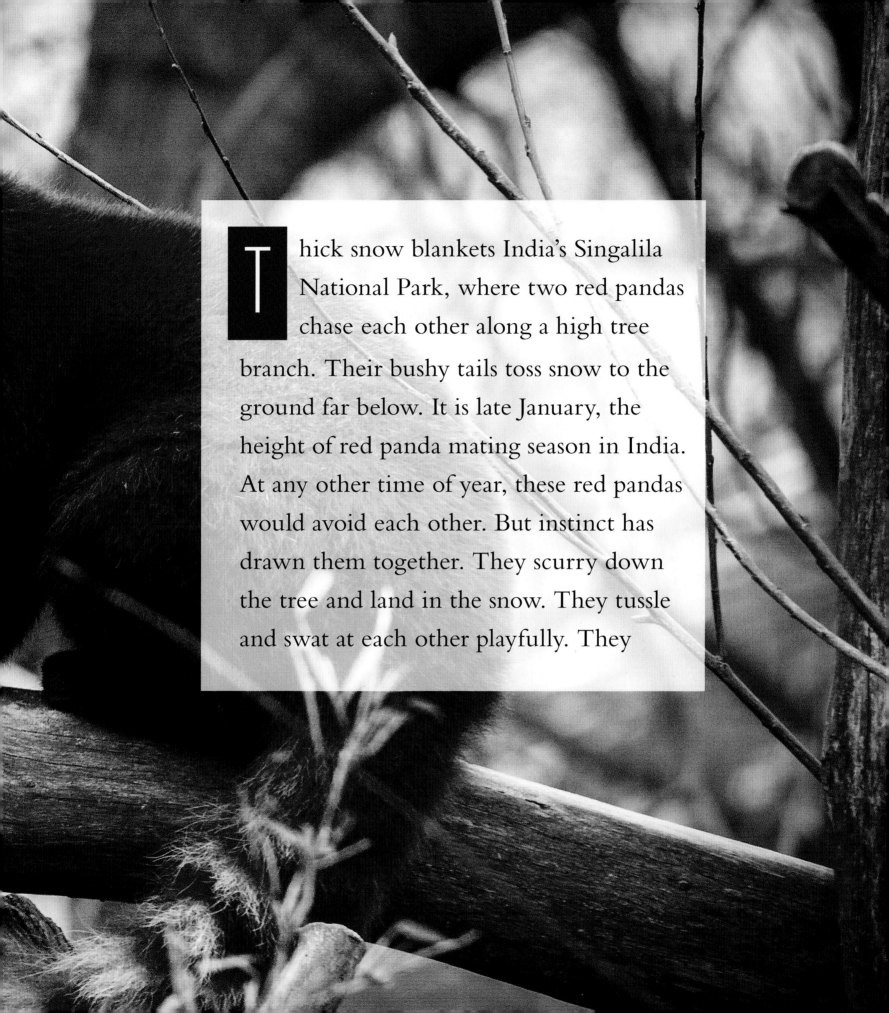

T hick snow blankets India's Singalila National Park, where two red pandas chase each other along a high tree branch. Their bushy tails toss snow to the ground far below. It is late January, the height of red panda mating season in India. At any other time of year, these red pandas would avoid each other. But instinct has drawn them together. They scurry down the tree and land in the snow. They tussle and swat at each other playfully. They

cuddle under the thick branches of a
yew tree. Then the female dashes away.
The male follows her, scampering over a
hollow log. The female has disappeared.
The male stops and looks around. He
cannot see her, but he can detect the
scent marks she has left behind. He
locates the female and together they roll
in the snow, making soft squeaks and
chirps. In the spring, the female with
give birth.

■ **Himalayan Red Panda**
Tibet, Bhutan, Nepal, and northeastern India

■ **Chinese Red Panda**
south-central China and northern Myanmar

Found in forested regions of the Himalayas, solitary red pandas generally keep to themselves, avoiding humans and other animals alike. These thick-furred animals retreat even higher up the mountains during warm summer months, but their way of life is becoming increasingly threatened. Both red panda subspecies are now endangered. The colored squares represent the areas where they still may be found in the wild today.

Red pandas are one of the few carnivores, or meat-eaters, that feed primarily on vegetation. Found before giant pandas, red pandas were the first to be called "pandas." (The word "panda" comes from a phrase meaning "eater of bamboo" in Nepalese.) Red and giant pandas are not related, though. Scientists once grouped red pandas with raccoons, but **genetic** research has determined otherwise. The red panda is far removed from its ancient raccoon cousins, and today it is a truly distinct species with no close living relatives. It is the only member of the family Ailuridae. The red panda's scientific name, *Ailurus fulgens*, comes from the Greek word for "cat" (*ailuros*) and the Latin *fulgeo*, or "shine," referring to a flash of lightning. This is why the red panda is sometimes called the fire cat. In China, it is known as a fire fox. Other nicknames include red cat-bear and lesser panda.

There are two recognized subspecies of red panda. *Ailurus fulgens styani*, called the Chinese red panda, is found in China and northern Myanmar. *Ailurus fulgens fulgens*, called the Himalayan red panda, is found in Tibet, Bhutan, Nepal, and northern India. The

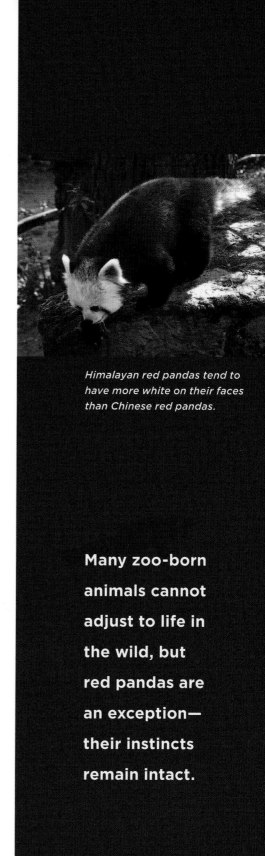

Himalayan red pandas tend to have more white on their faces than Chinese red pandas.

Many zoo-born animals cannot adjust to life in the wild, but red pandas are an exception— their instincts remain intact.

Female red pandas' home ranges are about one square mile (2.6 sq km), while males' home ranges are twice as big.

differences in the subspecies are subtle. The Himalayan red panda's fur, or pelage, is 1.5 to 2 inches (3.8–5.1 cm) long in winter, while the Chinese red panda's pelage can be nearly 3 inches (7.6 cm) long. The red panda's pelage is a rusty brown on the upper body that darkens to black on the limbs, rump, and underbelly. It has five to seven lighter-colored rings on its long, bushy tail—similar to a raccoon's tail. The Chinese subspecies has more black fur on its rump and hind parts and more distinct dark tail stripes. A red panda uses its tail for balance while climbing trees. It also uses its tail as a blanket in winter. Red pandas have white **muzzles** and markings on their cheeks and above their eyes. Their ears are also rimmed with white fur. The Chinese subspecies has a slightly larger head with more red on its face than the Himalayan subspecies, which has more white. Red pandas are typically about the size of a large housecat. They are 20 to 25 inches (50.8–63.5 cm) long from nose to rump. The tail can be nearly as long as the body. Weight depends on the environment and available food. Male red pandas vary from 8 to 14 pounds (3.6–6.4 kg), and females are slightly smaller.

Because male and female red pandas look the same, it is difficult to distinguish the animal's gender from a distance.

The red panda's pelage and tail are less bushy during warm summer months to help prevent overheating.

Red pandas are mammals. Mammals are animals that, with the exceptions of the egg-laying platypus and echidna, give birth to live young and produce milk to feed them. Like all mammals, red pandas are warm-blooded. This means that their bodies maintain a constant temperature that is usually warmer than their surroundings. Red pandas prefer low temperatures and high humidity, so they live in cool, rainy mountain forests at elevations of up to 7,000 feet (2,134 m) in winter and up to 11,500 feet (3,505 m) in summer. When the temperature gets too warm in summer, red pandas cool off by lying on their backs with their legs splayed out to let the heat escape past the thin fur on their bellies. In winter, their fur grows thicker to protect them from the cold. They sleep with their bushy tails wrapped around their bodies and faces.

Dense fur on the bottoms of their feet helps red pandas maintain their footing while traveling over wet, slippery branches, snow-covered ground, and icy rocks. Five clawed digits on each foot help them climb trees. Red pandas always climb down trees head first, gripping with their hind claws. Red pandas and giant pandas share

In 1869, the London Zoo became the first institution to house a red panda outside its natural habitat.

Without fruit or insects to supplement its diet, a red panda may lose up to 15 percent of its body weight in winter.

a trait that other animals lack: a false thumb. An extra-long wrist bone on each front paw works like a short thumb. Scientists believe giant pandas **evolved** with this trait in order to grip the bamboo plants they consume, while red pandas evolved with the false thumb to grip vines and branches as they traveled through the trees. The false thumb allows red pandas to not only climb narrow branches but also grip slender plant stems while feeding.

More than 90 percent of the red panda's diet is made up of bamboo leaves. They prefer the leaves of plants that are less than two years old. This is likely because young bamboo leaves contain about twice as much protein as bamboo stems and old leaves. There may be up to 40 different bamboo species in a red panda's habitat, but it typically feeds on just 1 or 2 of them. Red pandas may supplement their diet with the fruit of various brambles and occasionally flowers, seeds, eggs, and insects. Some will even consume birds and mice. In some parts of China, red pandas share habitat with giant pandas, which also eat bamboo. But there is little competition between the species. While giant pandas eat every part of the bamboo plant, red pandas eat only the leaves and shoots.

Members of the order Carnivora that eat mostly vegetation are called hypocarnivores.

Red pandas have a simple stomach and a short digestive tract, so food passes through the body quickly.

These make up only about a third of the giant panda's diet, leaving plenty of bamboo leaves for red pandas.

Red pandas have 36 to 38 teeth. Compared with other carnivores of a similar size, red pandas have exceptionally strong chewing muscles. Unlike giant pandas, which chomp mouthfuls of bamboo and swallow their food with little chewing, red pandas nip individual leaves from stems with great precision before thoroughly chewing each

mouthful. The saliva in their mouths aids digestion—
unlike most other mammals, red pandas do not have
special bacteria in their gut to help break down food. Red
pandas absorb only about 30 percent of the **nutrients** in
bamboo. They spend up to 14 hours a day eating, since
they need to consume nearly 3.5 pounds (1.6 kg) of fresh
bamboo leaves and almost 9 pounds (4.1 kg) of fresh shoots
a day to meet their minimum energy requirements.

Like giant pandas, red pandas use their thumb-like wrist bone to grip slender objects such as bamboo stalks.

Red pandas are solitary animals, meaning they live alone. Red pandas establish a home range and mark the boundaries of their territory with urine, **feces**, and an oily substance sprayed from a **gland** under their tails. The pads of their feet also leave scent marks. Unlike many other territorial animals, red pandas do not vigorously defend their home range from intruders. Most red pandas' home ranges overlap. Rather than fight, which would expend precious energy, they usually simply avoid each other. They may patrol less than 25 percent of their home range each month. Red pandas typically select habitats with many fallen logs and tree stumps. Studies have shown that red pandas feed from the ground only about 15 percent of the time. More often, they sit on branches, stumps, or fallen logs to better reach tall bamboo and plants. Red pandas also need to be near a water source, as they must drink fresh water every day.

Researchers disagree on when red pandas are most active. Some red pandas that were studied in China foraged and fed at dawn, dusk, and through the night. Others were more active during the day. Scientists think

Other animals whose diets depend on bamboo are giant pandas (above), Madagascar's bamboo lemurs, and bamboo rats of China and Southeast Asia.

Wheeting allows a mother to stay in contact with her cubs, even when she is foraging away from them.

Red pandas kept in zoos in the southern hemisphere breed from June to August and give birth between December and February.

that red pandas' behavior is tied to the number and types of predators in an area as well as the human activities that are present in their habitat. Regardless of when they forage and feed, red pandas are generally quiet animals. Only during rare aggressive encounters with each other do red pandas hiss or snort. Mating pairs emit a squeaky chattering sound that scientists call twittering. And if baby red pandas feel abandoned or stressed, they make a whistling sound similar to a bird call. Mother red pandas whistle back to let their offspring know their location. Researchers call this sound a wheet.

Rather than relying on vocal communication, red pandas use their keen sense of smell to avoid each other or locate mates. During mating season, from January to March, mature females' urine changes scent, signaling to males in the area that they are ready to mate. A male will follow his nose to the source of the scent and begin courtship with a receptive female. He will follow her around, sniffing her. He will twitter into her ear, and she will respond with squeaks. They will chase each other playfully and feed and sleep together for a few days. Each year, the female has a very small window of time during

which she can become pregnant: just 24 hours. After mating, the male returns to his home range, and the female prepares for motherhood.

The red panda's **gestation** period can vary from 98 to 158 days. Although little is known about red panda reproduction, scientists believe this wide range indicates that red pandas are capable of delayed implantation. This means that after the female red panda's eggs are fertilized, they turn into balls of cells that float in the female's

Red pandas in zoos live 10.5 years on average, but one named Jane lived to the age of 19 at the Sacramento Zoo.

uterus for a time before developing into red panda cubs. This allows a female red panda to prepare her body with enough food and also to give birth at a time of year when there will be sufficient nourishment for her offspring. Therefore, scientists believe changing climate conditions may affect red panda reproduction from year to year.

Before she gives birth, the female red panda selects a secluded nest site—usually a hole in a tall tree—where she and her offspring will be safest from predators. The female lines the den with soft plants, leaves, and moss.

Sometime between late May and early August, she gives birth to one or two cubs. Litters of three or four do occur, but they are rare. Weighing just four ounces (113 g), cubs are born blind, deaf, and covered with fluffy yellowish-gray fur that darkens with age. After two to three weeks, their eyes and ears open.

For the first three months of their lives, cubs are especially vulnerable. They remain hidden inside the nest, feeding on their mother's milk. They grow slowly, adding about one ounce (28.3 g) of weight every five days. When the cubs first venture outside, they stay on a branch close to the nest. As they get older, they get braver, and their mother helps them climb head first down the tree to explore the land below. Some cubs are anxious and scurry down with little assistance. Other cubs resist. Their mothers must grab hold with their mouths and drag them down to the ground. Together, mother and offspring feed on bamboo leaves. Until the cubs are about eight months old, they eat only leaves. Their digestive systems must fully develop before they can add other items to their diet.

If her cubs are born early enough in the summer, the youngsters will leave their mother's home range

Newborn red pandas weigh as much as a stick of butter; after two months, they weigh as much as a football.

A mother red panda sleeps on her back with her newborn cubs on her chest or belly for their first few weeks.

Clouded leopard hunting is banned in most countries, but such protective laws are poorly enforced.

before winter. Then the female red panda can mate again. Red pandas reach sexual maturity by age one or two and can potentially reproduce every year until they are about eight or nine years old. Red pandas can live to be 12 years old. However, given the natural threats of predators as well as human actions, wild red pandas rarely survive past age six. Scientists estimate that 86 percent of red panda cubs do not survive their first year of life, and more than 50 percent of adult red pandas perish long before they reach old age. The red panda's most dangerous predator is the clouded leopard. These cats weigh up to 50 pounds (22.7 kg). They can climb straight up a tree, jump nearly four feet (1.2 m), and use their sharp claws to creep upside down along tree branches, like a fly on the ceiling. Despite being 10 times smaller than a tiger, the clouded leopard has teeth about as long as a tiger's—approximately 2 inches (5.1 cm). Red pandas stand little chance against clouded leopards, but these cats are as rare as red pandas. Humans pose a greater threat to red pandas by **deforestation** and **poaching**. Red pandas are captured for the exotic pet trade and hunted for their beautiful fur.

Red pandas must be ever watchful for predators that rely on camouflage and stealth to sneak up on prey.

In the southwestern Chinese province of Yunnan, traditional hats made of red panda pelts can still be found today.

ADVENTURERS & ESCAPE ARTISTS

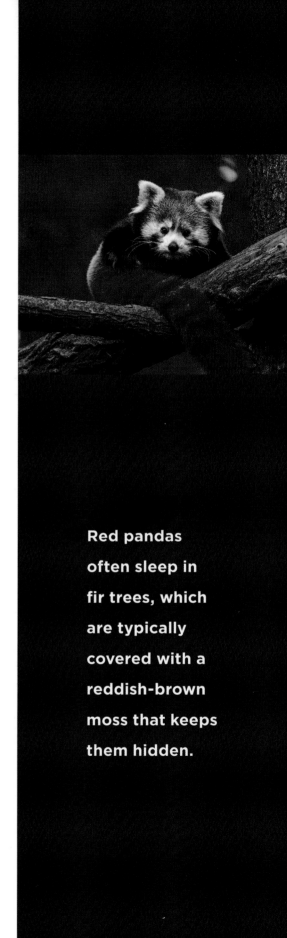

T he red panda has long played a role in the traditions of many **cultures** in its native lands. Some people in rural areas of northern Bhutan believe red pandas are bad luck and that seeing one is a sign that someone in the village will die. Such superstitions cause people to chase away or attempt to kill red pandas. However, in western Bhutan, people believe that seeing a red panda is a sign of good fortune, and in northeastern Bhutan, some think that when Buddhist monks die, their spirits live on as red pandas. In the Arunachal Pradesh region of India, people traditionally kept red panda tails as lucky charms. The Magar people of Nepal traditionally used red panda fur in the costumes of their spiritual leaders. The fur was believed to protect against evil spirits. Most practices involving red panda **pelts** and tails have faded since red pandas gained widespread legal protection in the 1990s, but some traditions continue to this day, leading to demand for poached red pandas. Among the Yi people of China, red panda fur hats are still worn by men at their weddings. They believe the hats will ensure a successful marriage.

Red pandas often sleep in fir trees, which are typically covered with a reddish-brown moss that keeps them hidden.

Red pandas groom themselves the same way cats do, keeping their coats clean and tidy at all times.

Red pandas do not lap up water but instead dip their front paws in water and then lick the water off their paws.

For the most part, red pandas are adored. The red panda has served as the state animal of Sikkim, India, since the early 1990s. It is also the mascot of the annual Darjeeling Tea Festival. In North American culture, red pandas are seen as cute, smart, and helpful critters. In the 2007 animated musical movie *Barbie as the Island Princess*, Sagi, a wise red panda, and Azul, a loud peacock, discover a little girl shipwrecked on their island after a storm. Sagi and a group of other animals help the girl, named Ro, and follow her on a series of adventures. Another wise red panda is a major character in DreamWorks' Kung Fu Panda franchise. Master Shifu first appeared in *Kung Fu Panda* in 2008. The Mandarin Chinese word *shīfu* means "old person of skill," such as a teacher. Master Shifu lives in the Jade Palace and teaches young martial artists. Through his patient guidance and training, Po, a clumsy giant panda, becomes a kung fu master himself and is dubbed the Dragon Warrior. Master Shifu's coloration (he is white with red markings instead of the reverse) is explained away by his advanced age: he is more than 70 years old.

The television series *Enviropals!* features Rae Rae the red panda. He lives in the fictional land of Naturia,

In the Kung Fu Panda movies, Master Shifu is the head teacher at the Jade Palace and trainer of many warriors.

where he and his friends teach viewers about solar power, gardening, fish hatcheries, geothermal energy, tree farms, and many other science-based topics. Many PBS stations carry *Enviropals!*, which was created by Shooting Star Educational Television in 2009. The 30-minute episodes can also be viewed online. A popular computer game featuring a red panda was created in 2008 by Red Panda Games. *Bipo: The Mystery of the Red Panda* is a puzzle-solving adventure game that features an anime red panda named Bipo. Bipo meets many characters, such as Mr. Shinbun the badger and Birdie the baker, as he figures his way out of a variety of challenging situations. *Red Panda*

THE PANDA

This richly coloured animal is rare in Szechuan, but more common in Yunnan. In the former province it occurs in the southwest corner beyond the Chiench'ang Valley, frequenting the forested and brush-clad country between 5,000 and 10,000 feet altitude. In Chungking, Sui Fu, Chengtu, and other cities the skin is often on sale.

In the shape of its head, short, broad face, and short ears this animal is very catlike; the claws too are partially retractile. The limbs are short and stout; the soles of the feet furry; the tail is 16 to 18 inches long; stout, cylindrical, and ringed at intervals like a civet-cat. The fur is long, soft, rich, dark, ferruginous on back, shoulders, and flanks; underparts, black; claws, white; soles of feet, greyish; forehead, chestnut with rufous stripe running down from the eye to near the snout; face, lips, edges, and inner surface of ears, white; outer surface of ears, dark red.

The Chinese Panda ranges from 38 to 44 inches, tip to tip, and weighs 9 to 10 pounds. It is darker and rather larger than the typical Himalayan species, and has been recognized as a distinct race under the name of *Ailurus fulgens styani*. Its colloquial name is "Chu-chieh-liang," which refers to the nine rings on the tail.

from A Naturalist in Western China*, by Ernest Henry Wilson (1876–1930)*

Run is a colorful online game created in 2012 by a group of students at the Centre for Digital Media in Vancouver, British Columbia. They partnered with the Red Panda Network (RPN) to promote donations to help save wild red pandas. Other online or mobile games that feature red pandas involve puzzles and arcade-style obstacles.

Real-life red pandas have had some adventurous journeys as well. At the Norfolk Zoo in Virginia, a red panda named Yin escaped from her enclosure twice in 2007. The first time, she simply ran up a tree and made a flying leap to freedom. The zoo then installed an electric wire fence at the top of her pen. But that did not stop Yin. A few weeks later, she leaped onto a branch that overhung the electric wire and ran off again. Yin was recaptured on zoo grounds, but in 2017, a red panda named Sunny escaped from the same enclosure and was never found. In 2008, mother red panda Pichu and her cub Isla escaped from the Galloway Wildlife Conservation Park in Scotland. They survived for two months at a nearby farm before being captured and returned to the zoo.

Rusty the red panda had been on exhibit at the Smithsonian National Zoo in Washington, D.C., for just

In 1997, Sweden issued a commemorative postage stamp featuring a Himalayan red panda.

When red pandas stick out their tongues, they are using tiny bumps under the tips of their tongues to collect scent.

three weeks when he escaped his enclosure on June 24, 2013. Heavy rains had pushed a tree branch down against the electric fence surrounding Rusty's enclosure, allowing the red panda to simply climb out. At 8:00 A.M., the zoo alerted keepers of a "Code Green," meaning an animal was on the loose. News of the missing red panda spread quickly on Twitter with the hashtag #findrusty. At 1:15 P.M., a family on vacation spotted Rusty in a tree about one mile (1.6 km) from the zoo. Officials rushed to the scene. Using a long pole, they nudged Rusty off a branch. He tumbled into a safety net, and by 2:00 P.M., he was back in his enclosure. Rusty has since fathered several cubs at the National Zoo.

Masala, a red panda at the Sequoia Park Zoo in Eureka, California, enjoyed freedom a little longer than Rusty. In November 2015, Masala scaled the fence of her enclosure and headed into a nearby wooded area. More than 200 volunteers combed the area in search of the 17-month-old red panda. Finally, after three days, Masala was spotted close to a street about half a mile (0.8 km) from the zoo. A volunteer searcher chased Masala up a tree and guarded her, keeping her safely off the street

until zoo officials arrived. Then it took about two hours to coax Masala out of the tree using bamboo treats. Zoos that keep red pandas must take special care in designing their enclosures. A notice to zookeepers from the Association of Zoos and Aquariums states, "Beware: red pandas are escape artists."

Abundant climbing structures and places to hide from people are important for red pandas to have in zoo enclosures.

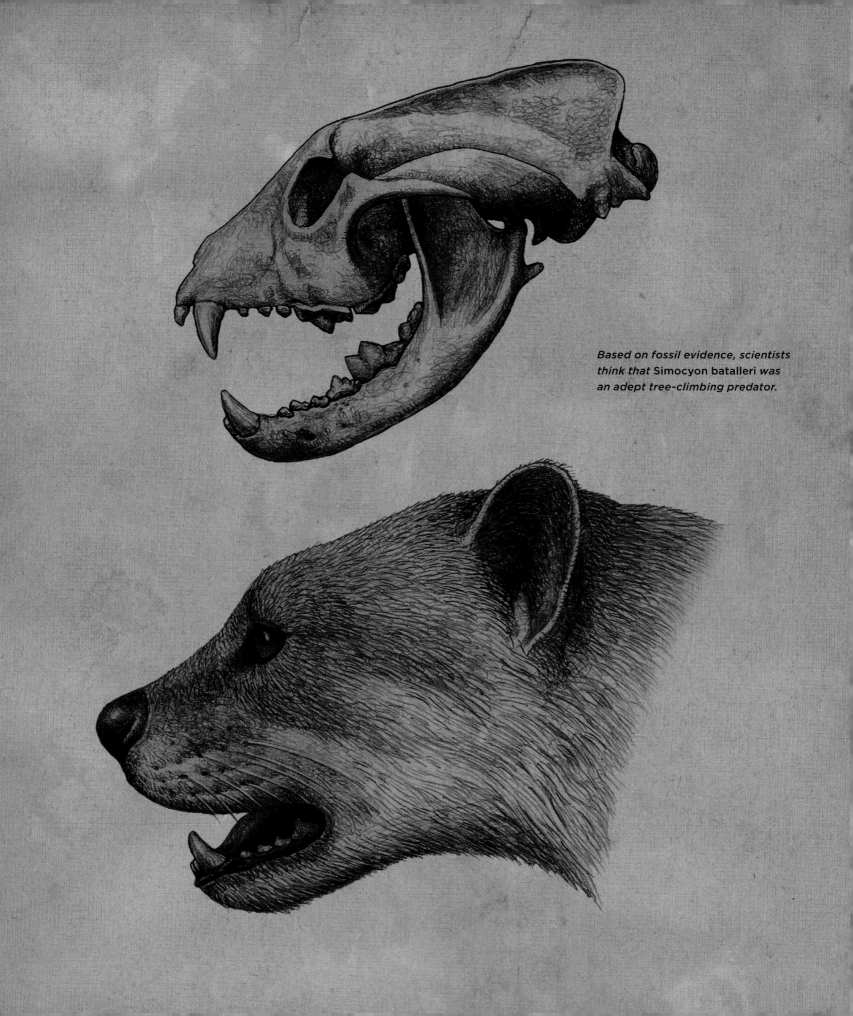

Based on fossil evidence, scientists think that Simocyon batalleri *was an adept tree-climbing predator.*

DANGER ZONE

S cientists believe all carnivores descended from a group of tree-dwelling, weaselly mammals called Miacids that existed about 60 million years ago. Miacids separated into Caniformia (ground-dwelling dogs and bears) and Feliformia (tree-dwelling cats and mongooses). The animals that would eventually evolve into red pandas broke away from the Feliforms about 38 million years ago. They continued to evolve into animals that foraged on the ground but slept in trees. The first red panda ancestors with the false thumb characteristic of today's animals were members of the genus *Simocyon*, or short-snouted dogs. They lived about 20 million years ago in what is now Europe. They were the size of cougars and had teeth and jaws capable of crushing bone. Another red panda relative was *Magerictis imperialensis*. It was similar in size to modern red pandas, but its diet was different. It ate a variety of plants, eggs, insects, and small animals. While the larger red panda ancestors died out, some of the smaller ones continued to thrive, moving to Asia and adopting a mostly vegetarian lifestyle in mountainous forests. Only one red panda

Prone to overheating in the summer, furry red pandas thrive in snowy winter weather.

Fossils have been found in Tennessee of a red panda ancestor that lived 7 to 4 million years ago.

Bamboo shoots are harvested for human food when they are about 12 inches (30.5 cm) tall—before they gain a bitter taste.

species ultimately survived the millennia and now exists as the sole member of its family.

Despite their long history, red pandas are now at serious risk of disappearing from the planet forever. In 2015, the International Union for Conservation of Nature (IUCN) listed the red panda as endangered. This means that red pandas are facing many threats that could lead to their **extinction**. The IUCN estimates that the red panda population has declined by more than 50 percent since 1960, and it expects red panda numbers to fall even faster over the next several decades, thanks to increased human activity in red panda habitats. The IUCN Red List of Threatened Species states that fewer than 10,000 red pandas exist in the wild. Scientists and conservationists working in red panda habitats put that number at around 2,000.

One of the major challenges red pandas face is habitat **fragmentation**. When large swaths of forests are destroyed, leaving only scattered patches, red pandas may not be able to reach each other to mate. In addition, because red pandas depend so heavily on bamboo, the loss of this food source can be devastating. Bamboo is a type of grass that

flowers once and then dies off. While new shoots can grow from a parent plant, if the land is degraded, the bamboo will not grow. Red panda forests are often cleared for logging and cattle pastures, particularly in India, where dairy cattle are raised for the nation's growing cheese industry. Hillside bamboo forests are also cleared for terrace farming in much of the red panda's range.

As humans **encroach** on red panda habitat, they bring dogs that become fierce predators of red pandas. The

Red pandas are selective in their food sources, choosing young leaves and shoots that are full of energy-rich nutrients.

Despite their docile nature, red pandas are unpredictable wild animals and should not be kept as pets.

dogs also carry a disease called canine distemper, which can spread to red pandas. Dogs can be **vaccinated** against the disease, but the vaccine does not work on red pandas. Scientists fear that outbreaks of canine distemper among red pandas could take out entire groups of these animals. Another threat to red pandas is the exotic pet trade. Because of their cute appearance and gentle disposition, red pandas have long been popular pets. In 1972, the Indian government made it illegal to possess red pandas. But this has not stopped the trade. Poachers also kill red pandas for their meat as well as for their pelts, which are used to make traditional hats in China and Bhutan. The organs of red pandas are used in Chinese folk medicine.

Since the first account of red pandas was published by French zoologist Frédéric Cuvier in 1825, red pandas have been kept in captivity. The red panda's diet and biological processes were not well understood at first. Not realizing that red pandas are mostly vegetarian, some zoos tried to feed them beef, chicken, and eggs. Even plant-based diets were unsuccessful, since bamboo leaves were not provided in proper quantities. Most zoos were unable to keep red pandas alive for very long. By the 1960s, keepers had learned through trial and error how to better feed and care for red pandas. However, they were still living only a fraction of their normal life span. But recognizing their rarity in the wild, people continued trying to **captive-breed** them. Today, many aspects of red pandas' lives are still a mystery, but at least the animals are now living longer in captivity. Unfortunately, however, scientists estimate that less than one-third of the red pandas kept in zoos are reproducing as much as they normally would in the wild. And of the red pandas born

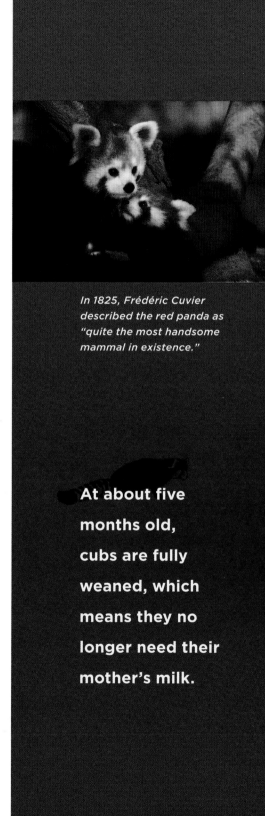

In 1825, Frédéric Cuvier described the red panda as "quite the most handsome mammal in existence."

At about five months old, cubs are fully weaned, which means they no longer need their mother's milk.

Unlike many small mammals that drink from gravity bottles in zoos, red pandas prefer dishes of water.

A 2009 study revealed that red pandas offered a choice of plain or sweetened water preferred the sweet option.

in captivity, about 50 percent die within their first nine months of life.

A step toward better understanding wild red pandas came in 2006. Dr. Sunita Pradhan, formerly of the Padmaja Naidu Himalayan Zoological Park in Darjeeling, India, is the world's leading red panda **ecologist**. She and a team of Indian filmmakers made a documentary called *Cherub of the Mist* (2006). It featured two female red pandas named Mini and Sweety who had been born in captivity and became the first red pandas to take part in a reintroduction program. The red pandas were fitted with **radio collars** that Dr. Pradhan could track. Then they were released into the Singalila National Park in India. As Dr. Pradhan followed Mini and Sweety, her team spotted a wild red panda and caught its mating, nesting, and birthing behaviors on film. It was the first time anyone had ever witnessed these behaviors in the wild.

Protecting red pandas in their native habitat is vital to saving the species. The RPN is an organization made up of biologists, environmental scientists, and forest rangers who work together to protect red pandas in the wild. Headquartered in Nepal, the RPN educates people

about the importance of preserving the shrinking forests of Nepal. They coordinate with community leaders to develop reforestation plans, and they train local people to monitor endangered wildlife. While conservationists' work has helped reveal many of the red panda's secrets, continued efforts to better understand the natural behaviors of red pandas are urgently needed if we are to save this adorable and amazing animal from extinction.

Being small prey animals with few defenses, red pandas are curious but also naturally cautious animals.

ANIMAL TALE: HOW RED PANDA SAVED THE PEOPLE

Few stories of red pandas appear in the folklore of their homeland. But long ago, when red pandas were abundant in Pakistan, a legend emerged of how the red panda stole fire from the trees and shared it with people.

In the old days, the only one who knew the secret of fire was the divine cedar tree. But he refused to share the secret with anyone. When the cold wind blew fiercely down from the mountains, the people wished they knew the secret of fire.

One especially brutal winter, the people went to the wild goat called the markhor and said, "Please climb to the top of the mountain where the divine cedar tree dwells and get the secret of fire for us. We are so cold we will surely not last through the winter."

So Markhor, with his shaggy coat and long, spiral horns, climbed to the top of the mountain where the cedar trees stood together. He marched up to the divine one and said, "You have kept the secret of fire to yourself for too long. I ask that you share it with the people, for they will surely die without it."

"No!" shouted the tree. "We are not concerned. Now go away."

Markhor went back to the people. "I am sorry," he said, "but I could not reason with the divine cedar tree. I could not get the secret of fire for you."

The people next went to the snow leopard. "Please," they begged, "climb to the top of the mountain and get the secret of fire for us."

So Snow Leopard, with his thick fur and long, fluffy tail, climbed the mountain and said to the divine cedar tree, "You have kept the secret of fire long enough. You must share it with the people or I will claw and bite your bark and branches."

"No!" shouted the tree. "We are not afraid of you. Now go away."

Snow Leopard returned to the people. "I am sorry," he said, "but I could not frighten the divine cedar tree. I could not get the secret of fire for you."

Finally, the people went to Red Panda. "Please get the secret of fire for us," they implored.

So Red Panda, wearing his mask and mittens, climbed the mountain. He hunched down in the snow and waited. When the moon was high in the night sky, the divine cedar tree reached down inside his roots and pulled out a heap of smoldering coals. He set them on the ground and waved his branches, fanning the coals. The coals turned red-hot. The trees began to dance. That's when Red Panda sneaked up and snatched a coal. The trees gave chase, but Red Panda was too quick. In a flash, he disappeared down the mountain.

Handing over the hot coal, Red Panda said to the people, "I'm sorry that I had to steal the secret of fire, but now you will survive the winter." The people thanked Red Panda and called him the fire fox—the sly one who steals fire.

To this day, the deodar cedar is considered a sacred tree by many Buddhists in the Himalayan region. And while the red panda is no longer found in Pakistan, its descendants in other parts of Asia are still known as fire foxes.

GLOSSARY

captive-breed – to breed and raise in a place from which escape is not possible

cultures – particular groups in a society that share behaviors and characteristics that are accepted as normal by those groups

deforestation – the clearing away of trees from a forest

ecologist – a person who studies the relationships of organisms living together in an environment

encroach – to move into an area already occupied

evolved – gradually developed into a new form

extinction – the act or process of becoming extinct; coming to an end or dying out

feces – waste matter eliminated from the body

fragmentation – the breaking up of an organism's habitat into scattered sections that may result in difficulty moving safely from one place to another

genetic – relating to genes, the basic physical units of heredity

gestation – the period of time it takes a baby to develop inside its mother's womb

gland – an organ in a human or animal body that produces chemical substances used by other parts of the body

muzzles – the projecting parts of animals' faces that include the nose and mouth

nutrients – substances that give a living thing energy and help it grow

pelts – the skins of animals with the fur or wool still attached

poaching – hunting protected species of wild animals, even though doing so is against the law

radio collars – collars fitted with small electronic devices that send signals to radio receivers

uterus – the organ in a female mammal's body where offspring develop before birth; another word for "womb"

vaccinated – given a substance to provide protection from a disease

SELECTED BIBLIOGRAPHY

"About the Red Panda." Red Panda Network. http://redpandanetwork.org/red_panda/about-the-red-panda/.

"*Ailurus fulgens*." The IUCN Red List of Threatened Species. http://www.iucnredlist.org/details/714/0.

Bedi, Naresh. *Cherub of the Mist*. DVD. New Dehli: Bedi Brothers Productions, 2006.

Glatston, Angela R., ed. *Red Panda: Biology and Conservation of the First Panda*. Amsterdam: Academic Press, 2011.

Macdonald, David W., ed. *The Princeton Encyclopedia of Mammals*. Princeton, N.J.: Princeton University Press, 2009.

"Red Panda." Smithsonian's National Zoo & Conservation Biology Institute. https://nationalzoo.si.edu/animals/red-panda.

Red pandas are occasionally aggressive toward one another, standing on their hind legs and batting with their forepaws.

INDEX